Cool

SNACK FOOD ART

Easy Recipes That Make Food Fun to Eat!

Nancy Tuminelly

ABDO
Publishing Company

To Adult Helpers

This is not your ordinary cookbook! Sure, we've provided ingredients lists and how-to photographs. But like any artistic endeavor, food art is all about creativity! Encourage kids to come up with their own ideas. Get creative with ingredients too. Scan your fridge and get started with whatever you have!

Always supervise kids when they are working in the kitchen. Food art often requires a lot of knife work such as slicing and shaping. Assist young artists whenever they are using knives. Occasionally, kids will need to use the oven or stovetop too. Be there to help when necessary, but encourage them to do as much as they can on their own. Kids love to share and eat their own creations!

Expect your young food artists to make a mess, but also expect them to clean up after themselves. Show them how to properly store unused ingredients. Most importantly, be a voice of encouragement. You might even get kids to eat healthy foods they've never had before!

Visit us at www.abdopublishing.com

Published by ABDO Publishing Company, 8000 West 78th Street, Edina, Minnesota 55439. Copyright © 2011 by Abdo Consulting Group, Inc. International copyrights reserved in all countries. No part of this book may be reproduced in any form without written permission from the publisher. Checkerboard Library™ is a trademark and logo of ABDO Publishing Company.

Printed in the United States of America, North Mankato, Minnesota
062010
092010

 PRINTED ON RECYCLED PAPER

Editor: Liz Salzmann
Series Concept: Nancy Tuminelly
Cover and Interior Design: Anders Hanson, Mighty Media, Inc.
Photo Credits: Anders Hanson, Shutterstock

The following manufacturers/names appearing in this book are trademarks: PAM®, Pillsbury® Creamy Supreme®, Pillsbury® Recipe Creations®, Proctor-Silex®

Library of Congress Cataloging-in-Publication Data

Tuminelly, Nancy, 1952-
  Cool snack food art : easy recipes that make food fun to eat! / Nancy Tuminelly.
      p. cm. -- (Cool food art)
  Includes index.
  ISBN 978-1-61613-367-2
  1. Snack foods--Juvenile literature. 2. Food presentation--Juvenile literature. I. Title.
  TX740.T84 2010
  641.5'39--dc22
                            2010003573

CONTENTS

Play with Your Food! 4

The Basics 5

The Coolest Ingredients 8

The Tool Box 10

Cooking Terms 11

Techniques 12

Speedy Snack **14**

Beach Ball Cheese Ball **16**

Bug Bites **18**

Chili Snake Dogs **20**

Peanut Butter and Candy Pizza **22**

Sunflower Surprise **24**

Kookie Katerpillar **26**

Sweet Treat Flowerpots **28**

Wrap It Up! 30

Glossary 31

Web Sites 31

Index 32

PAGE 14

PAGE 18

PAGE 22

PAGE 26

PLAY WITH YOUR FOOD!

Unless Mom says not to!

It's time to play with your food! Get ready to make faces, flowers, animals, and bugs! You're an artist now. The plate is your **canvas**, and your favorite foods are your paints!

As you make your cool snack food art, be open to all sorts of ingredients. You can use anything! Fresh fruits and vegetables work great. You can shape and slice them in so many ways! Use foods that you like, but don't be afraid to try new things.

Like any kind of art, food art is about **expression** and creativity. Get inspired and give each dish your own special touch. A lot of cookbooks teach you how to make food that tastes great. This book will inspire you to make snacks that taste and look great!

THE BASICS

Get started with a few important basics

ASK PERMISSION

> Before you cook, get permission to use the kitchen, cooking tools, and ingredients.

> You might want an adult to help you with some of your creations. But if you want to do something yourself, say so!

> When you need help, just ask. An adult should always be around when you are using sharp knives, the oven, or the stove.

BE PREPARED

> Read through the recipe before you begin.

> Get organized. Have your tools and ingredients ready before you start.

> Think of **alternative** ingredients if you want!

BE SMART, BE SAFE

➤ Never work in the kitchen when you are home alone!

➤ Have an adult nearby when you are using sharp tools such as a knife, peeler, or grater. Always use sharp tools with care. Use a cutting board when you are working with a knife.

➤ Work slowly and carefully. Great food art rarely happens when you rush!

BE NEAT AND CLEAN

➤ Start with clean hands, clean tools, and a clean work surface.

➤ Always wash fruits and vegetables. Rinse them under cold water. Pat them dry with a towel. Then they won't slip when you cut them.

➤ Tie back long hair so it stays out of the way and out of the food!

➤ Wear comfortable clothes that can get a little bit dirty. Roll up your sleeves.

Note on Measuring

The recipes in this book provide **approximations**. Feel free to be creative! For example, a recipe may call for 1 tablespoon of cream cheese. Do you like cream cheese? Then add more! If you don't like cream cheese, then try something else!

SHOPPING FOR PRODUCE

Sometimes canned produce works perfectly in your food art. But more often than not, fresh fruits and vegetables are better. When you are shopping for your food art groceries, think about what you are making. For example, do you want a really big cucumber or a small one? Fruits and vegetables come in all different shapes and sizes! Think about the shapes and sizes that will work best in your food art.

SAVING INGREDIENTS

When you are making food art, sometimes you only need a little bit of something. That means you have to do a good job of putting things away so they stay fresh. Cover leftover ingredients so that they will keep. Airtight containers work best. You don't want to waste a lot of food!

KEY SYMBOLS

In this book, you will see some symbols beside the recipes. Here is what they mean.

Sharp!
You need to use a knife for this recipe. Ask an adult to stand by.

Hot!
This activity requires the use of an oven or stove. You need adult supervision. Always use oven mitts when holding hot pans.

THE COOLEST

KETCHUP

MUSTARD

RANCH DRESSING

COOKING SPRAY

CHOPPED BACON

SMOKED SAUSAGE LINKS

HOT DOG

STRING CHEESE

SLICED CHEDDAR CHEESE

SHREDDED CHEDDAR CHEESE

CREAM CHEESE

SOUR CREAM

PRETZEL STICKS

ONION SOUP MIX

CRACKERS

CHOW MEIN NOODLES

SEAMLESS DOUGH SHEET

CHILI

PEANUT BUTTER

SUNFLOWER SEEDS

CHERRY TOMATOES

RICE CAKE

8

INGREDIENTS

WHITE FROSTING

REFRIGERATED
COOKIE DOUGH

CHOCOLATE SANDWICH
COOKIES

LOLLIPOPS

CARAMELS

MINI MARSHMALLOWS

FOOD COLORING

FRUIT LEATHER ROLL

PULL AND PEEL
LICORICE

SMALL CANDY
PIECES

CHOCOLATE-COVERED
PRETZEL ROUNDS

YOGURT-COATED
FRUIT BITES

GUMMY WORMS

GUMMY BEARS

SHREDDED
COCONUT

ORANGES

BELL PEPPERS

BLACK OLIVES

GREEN OLIVES WITH
PIMIENTO

PARSLEY

CUCUMBERS

BABY CARROTS

CARROTS

CELERY

MIXED GREENS

THE TOOL BOX

Here are some tools you'll need for most food art recipes

PARING KNIFE

SMALL SPATULA

SCISSORS

MINI MUFFIN PAN
AND PAPERS

BAKING SHEET

ALUMINUM FOIL

PLASTIC BAGS

ROUND BAKING SHEET

PLASTIC WRAP

MIXER AND BEATERS

MIXING BOWLS

CUTTING BOARD

COOKING TERMS

A simple list of words you'll want to know

CHOPPING

Chop means to cut things into small pieces. The more you chop, the smaller the pieces. If a recipe says finely chopped, it means you need very small pieces.

CUTTING LENGTHWISE

To cut something lengthwise means to cut *along* its length. You create pieces that are the *same length* as they were initially.

SLICING

Slice means to cut something into thin pieces. Each slice should be about the same thickness.

CUTTING CROSSWISE

To cut something crosswise means to cut *across* its length. The pieces will be shorter, but the *same width* as they were initially.

TECHNIQUES

Tips for making great food art

MAKING FACES

Food art is all about creativity. The recipes in this book will get you started. But your imagination is really the secret ingredient! A recipe may call for black olives as the eyes. But why not try raisins instead? Use these techniques for inspiration. Add your personal style to create cool variations!

Eyes

GRAPE HALVES ON
MARSHMALLOWS

BLACK OLIVE SLICES
ON CREAM CHEESE

BLUEBERRIES ON
BANANA SLICES

BLACK OLIVES ON
HARD-BOILED EGGS

Noses

CANTALOUPE BALL

BABY CARROT

RAISIN

GRAPE TOMATO

Mouths

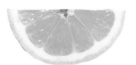

HALF A LEMON SLICE

RED BELL PEPPER TOP

ORANGE SECTION

GREEN PEPPER SLICE

ATTACHING WITH GOOEY STUFF

Food art combines a variety of ingredients. How do you hold them all together? Ingredients such as peanut butter, frosting, ketchup, and cream cheese can be used like glue. Plus, they taste great!

DRAWING WITH FOOD

You can decorate your food art just like the professionals decorate cakes! Put a **condiment** into a zippered plastic bag. Then cut off one of the corners at the bottom of the bag. Don't cut off too much. Now you can gently squeeze the bag to make drawings and **designs**.

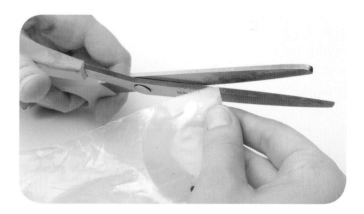

SCRAPING A BOWL

When using a mixer, turn off the mixer occasionally. Then scrape the sides and bottom of the bowl with a silicone spatula. That way you'll be sure that all of the ingredients are completely mixed. Recipes don't usually mention this important step. You just have to remember to do it!

SPEEDY
SNACK

Scoot this snack right into your tummy!

INGREDIENTS

4 pretzel sticks

1 stick string cheese

4 cucumber slices

1 cherry tomato, halved

2 black olives, halved

1 green olive with pimiento, halved

cream cheese

1 slice cheddar cheese

mixed greens

TOOLS

cutting board

paring knife

1 Stick a pretzel stick through each end of the string cheese.

2 Push a cucumber slice onto the ends of each pretzel stick for wheels.

3 On the back wheels, push a cherry tomato half onto the ends of the pretzel stick for hubcaps.

4 On the front wheels, use the closed halves of two black olives for hubcaps.

5 Push a pretzel stick into the top of the string cheese between the front wheels. Put a dab of cream cheese on top of the pretzel stick. Lay a pretzel stick across the cream cheese for handlebars.

6 Put a dab of cream cheese on the back of a green olive half. **Attach** the olive half to the front of the handlebars. Make sure the pimiento faces out. This is the headlight.

7 Place the cheddar cheese slice on a plate for a bike path. Put mixed greens on each side of the cheese for grass. Place the scooter on top of cheese path.

15

BEACH BALL
CHEESE BALL

Remember, no swimming for 30 minutes after you eat!

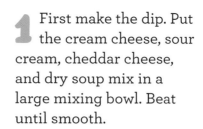

MAKES 1 BEACH BALL

INGREDIENTS

2 8-ounce packages cream cheese, softened

8 ounces sour cream

1 cup of shredded cheddar cheese

½ packet of dry onion soup mix

1 carrot, chopped

1 red bell pepper, chopped

1 yellow bell pepper, chopped

4 tablespoons black olives, chopped

4 tablespoons bacon, chopped

4 tablespoons parsley, chopped

crackers

TOOLS

measuring spoon & cup

mixing bowls

mixer and beaters

plastic wrap

paring knife

cutting board

small spatula

1 First make the dip. Put the cream cheese, sour cream, cheddar cheese, and dry soup mix in a large mixing bowl. Beat until smooth.

2 Line a small bowl with plastic wrap. Put the dip into the lined bowl. Chill in the refrigerator for 30 minutes. This is a good time to chop the other ingredients.

3 Take the dip out of the refrigerator. Put a serving plate over the bowl. Turn the plate and bowl over together. Lift the bowl off of the dip. Remove the plastic wrap. Use a spatula to smooth the dip into a round shape.

4 Use a knife to draw six equal sections onto the ball.

5 Sprinkle each section with one of the toppings and press lightly. Serve with crackers.

17

BUG
BITES

These bite-sized bugs are beyond tasty!

INGREDIENTS

8-ounce can seamless dough sheet

24 smoked sausage links

chow mein noodles

ketchup

mustard

ranch dressing

TOOLS

paring knife

cutting board

baking sheet

plastic bags

scissors

1 Preheat the oven to 375 degrees. Unroll the **dough**. Cut it into strips that are 1 inch (2.5 cm) wide and 3 inches (7.5 cm) long.

2 Wrap a smoked sausage link in each strip of dough. Pinch to seal.

3 Put the wrapped sausages on a baking sheet. Bake for 11 to 14 minutes, or until golden brown. Remove them from the baking sheet and let them cool.

4 Stick three chow mein noodles into each side of the bugs. These are the legs. Stick two noodles into each sausage link for antennas.

5 Fill one plastic bag with ketchup and one with mustard. Cut off a tiny corner of each bag.

6 Squeeze the mustard bag to make faces on the sausage links.

7 Decorate the bodies with ketchup and mustard.

8 Fill a small bowl with ranch dressing. Set the bugs and bowl of dressing on a serving **platter**.

CHILI
SNAKE DOGS

These silly snack snakes will melt in your mouth!

INGREDIENTS

8-ounce can seamless dough sheet

8 hot dogs

16 ounces chili

2 green olives with pimiento

1 red bell pepper

mixed greens

TOOLS

paring knife

cutting board

aluminum foil

scissors

baking sheet

1 Preheat the oven to 375 degrees. Unroll the **dough**. Fold it in half to make the dough extra thick. Cut the dough into strips that are 1 inch (2.5 cm) wide and 10 inches (25 cm) long.

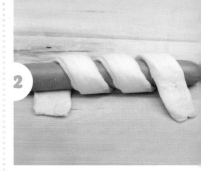

2 Wrap a dough strip around each hot dog. Leave 1 inch (2.5 cm) of dough at each end.

3 Cut 16 3-inch squares and 8 2-inch squares of aluminum foil. Roll each square into a ball.

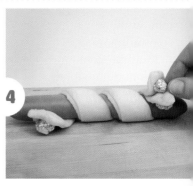

4 Cut a **slit** in one end of the dough on each snake to make a mouth. Put a small foil ball into each mouth. Prop up the heads and tails with the larger foil balls.

5 Put the snakes on a baking sheet. Bake for 14 to 17 minutes. While they are baking, heat the chili. Spoon the hot chili onto plates.

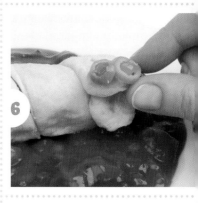

6 Take the snakes out of the oven. Remove all the foil balls. Put each snake on a plate of chili. Slice the green olives thinly. Put two slices on each head for eyes.

7 Cut strips of red bell pepper for tongues. Stick one into each mouth. Put mixed greens around each plate.

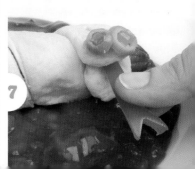

PEANUT BUTTER AND
CANDY PIZZA

As if pizza wasn't already delicious!

INGREDIENTS

18-ounce package
refrigerated
peanut butter
cookie dough

8 ounces white
frosting

20 drops red food
coloring

chocolate-
covered pretzel
rounds

yogurt-coated
fruit bites

gummy worms

gummy bears

shredded coconut

TOOLS

round baking
sheet

small mixing
bowl

knife

1 Set the cookie **dough** out until it is room temperature. This will make it easier to spread. Preheat the oven to 350 degrees.

2 Spread dough out evenly on a 12-inch round baking pan. Leave 1 inch (2.5 cm) around the edge. The dough needs room to **expand** as it bakes. This will be the "crust."

3 Bake the crust for 15 minutes or until golden brown. Remove it from the oven. Let it cool completely.

4 In a small bowl, mix the food coloring and frosting. This will be the "sauce."

5 Spread the sauce evenly over the crust.

6 Arrange your favorite colorful candies on the pizza. These are the "toppings."

7 Sprinkle shredded coconut over the top. This is the "cheese." Cut the pizza into pieces with a knife. Enjoy!

SUNFLOWER
SURPRISE

A flowery treat to brighten your day!

INGREDIENTS

1 rice cake

3 tablespoons
peanut butter

1 tablespoon
sunflower seeds

6 baby carrots

1 celery stalk

1 orange slice,
halved

mixed greens

TOOLS

measuring spoon

cutting board

paring knife

1 Cover the top of the rice cake with peanut butter. Sprinkle sunflower seeds on top of the peanut butter.

2 Cut the baby carrots in half lengthwise. Arrange them around the outside of the rice cake.

3 Add the celery stalk for the stem. Place orange slices on each side of the celery for leaves.

4 Put mixed greens around the base of the flower.

A SWEETER SURPRISE

In the mood for something sweet? Try a different version with these ingredients.

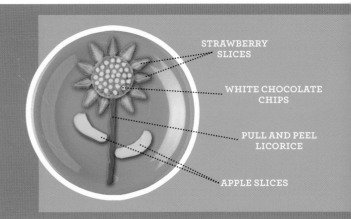

STRAWBERRY SLICES

WHITE CHOCOLATE CHIPS

PULL AND PEEL LICORICE

APPLE SLICES

KOOKIE
KATERPILLAR

Eat this treat before it turns into a butterfly!

INGREDIENTS

18-ounce package refrigerated chocolate chip cookie dough

8 ounces white frosting

8 drops green food coloring

pull and peel licorice

1 mini marshmallow

2 small candy pieces

TOOLS

baking sheet

small bowl

paring knife

cutting board

1 Bake the cookies according to the directions on the package. Allow them to cool. In a small bowl, mix the food coloring and frosting.

2 Cover the tops of the cookies with green frosting. Leave one cookie plain. Stack them in piles.

3 Combine the piles into one big stack. Put the plain cookie on top. Turn the stack on its side.

4 Cut 14 2-inch strips of pull and peel licorice. Push six into the frosting on each side for the legs. Stick two behind the head for antennas.

5 Cut the marshmallow in half. Use frosting to **attach** a candy piece to each half. Use frosting to attach the marshmallow eyes to the face.

DANGEROUSLY GOOD

In the mood for something spooky? Try a scary version with these ingredients.

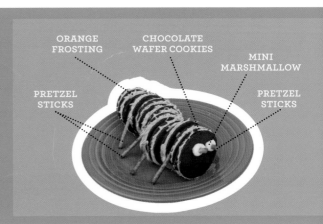

ORANGE FROSTING

CHOCOLATE WAFER COOKIES

MINI MARSHMALLOW

PRETZEL STICKS

PRETZEL STICKS

SWEET TREAT
FLOWERPOTS

It takes about an hour to grow these flowers!

INGREDIENTS

cooking spray

8 ounces refrigerated sugar cookie dough

12 caramels

⅓ cup crushed chocolate sandwich cookies

1 fruit leather roll, green

12 lollipops

TOOLS

mini muffin pan

mini muffin papers (optional)

paring knife

cutting board

1 Preheat the oven to 350 degrees. Coat the mini muffin pan with cooking spray. Or use mini muffin papers.

2 Separate the **dough** into 12 equal balls. Flatten the balls. Line each muffin cup with a flattened ball of dough. Spread the dough up the sides of the cups. Place a caramel in each cup.

3 Bake 10 to 12 minutes, or until the edges are golden brown. Allow the pan to cool completely.

4 Remove the cookies from the pan. Set them on a plate.

5 Fill the cookies with cookie crumbs.

6 Cut 12 long triangles out of fruit leather. Twist each one in the middle. Wrap them around the lollipop sticks.

7 Press the lollipop sticks into the caramels.

WRAP IT UP!

Food art finale!

Now you're ready to **design** your own snack food art! It helps to have a plan before you start. Make a quick **sketch** of your idea. Add notes about what ingredients will work best. Talk about your sketch with others. You will get great ideas! Make sure you get the camera out and take a photograph of your creation. The better your snack looks, the more likely it is to be eaten!

It's good to learn about food. The foods we eat have a lot to do with how we feel. The more familiar you are with the food around you, the better! Learning to make food teaches us about **nutrition** and health. Learning to make food art teaches us to have fun at the same time!

GLOSSARY

ALTERNATIVE – different from the original.

APPROXIMATION – about the right amount.

ATTACH – to join two things together.

CANVAS – a type of thick cloth that artists paint on.

CONDIMENT – something that adds flavor to food, such as a sauce or a spice.

DESIGN – 1. a decorative pattern or arrangement. 2. to plan how something will appear or work.

DOUGH – a thick mixture of flour, water, and other ingredients used in baking.

EXPAND – to become larger.

EXPRESSION – creating a work of art as a way to show one's feelings.

NUTRITION – how different foods affect one's health.

PLATTER – a large plate.

SKETCH – a drawing.

SLIT – a narrow cut or opening.

Web Sites

To learn more about cool food art, visit ABDO Publishing Company on the World Wide Web at **www.abdopublishing.com.** Web sites about cool food art are featured on our Book Links page. These links are routinely monitored and updated to provide the most current information available.

INDEX

A

Adult help (for safety), 5, 6, 7
Attaching (of ingredients), 13

B

Buying (of ingredients), 7

C

Candy (food art made with), 22–23, 26–27, 28–29
Cheese (food art made with), 14–15, 16–17
Chili (food art made with), 20–21
Chopping, 11
Cleanliness, 6
Clothing (while making food art), 6
Cookies/Cookie dough (food art made with), 22–23, 26–27, 28–29
Cooking terms, 11
Crackers, 16–17
Cream cheese (food art made with), 16–17
Creativity (with food), 4, 7, 12, 30
Cutting, 11

D

Dips, 18–19
Dough sheets (food art made with), 18–19, 20–21. *See also* Cookies/ Cookie dough
Drawing (with food), 13

F

Faces (as food art), 12, 20–21, 26–27
Frosting (food art made with), 22–23, 26–27
Fruits
buying, 7
food art made with, 4, 7, 24–25
washing, 6

H

Hair (while making food art), 6
Hot dogs (food art made with), 20–21

I

Ingredients, 8–9
buying, 7
measuring, 6
preparing, 5, 6, 30
storing, 7
types of, 4, 5, 8–9, 30
washing, 6

K

Knives
safety with, 5, 6, 7
uses of, 11

M

Measuring (of ingredients), 6
Mixing (of ingredients), 13

N

Nutrition, 30

O

Oven use, 5, 7

P

Peanut butter (food art made with), 22–23, 24–25
Permission (for kitchen use), 5
Photographs (of food art), 30
Pizza, 22–23
Preparation (for making food art), 5, 6, 30

Pretzels (food art made with), 14–15, 22–23

R

Recipe (reading of), 5
Rice cakes (food art made with), 24–25

S

Safety, 5, 6, 7
Sausage links (food art made with), 18–19
Scraping (of mixing bowl), 13
Sketches (of food art), 30
Slicing, 11
Soup mix (food art made with), 16–17
Sour cream (food art made with), 16–17
Storage (of ingredients), 7
Stove use, 5, 7
Sunflower seeds (food art made with), 24–25

T

Techniques (for making food art), 12–13

Terms (about cooking), 11
Tools, 10
preparing, 5
safety with, 6
types of, 10
washing, 6

V

Vegetables
buying, 7
food art made with, 4, 7, 14–15, 16–17, 20–21, 24–25
washing, 6

W

Washing (of hands, ingredients, and tools), 6